DEFENSE INDUSTRY CAREERS

Gregory L. Pitt

DEFENSE INDUSTRY CAREERS

Copyright © 2014 by Gregory L. Pitt

Cover design by Goodlife Guide
Printed in the United States of America

First Printing: 2014

★

INTRODUCTION

D efense and military contracting is a multibillion dollar industry that continues to grow at a rapid pace. Defense contracting and military contracting companies provide human resources, goods, products, and services in support of the U.S. government and the U.S. military both at home and abroad. This industry is job plentiful and the need for qualified employees continues to increase. There are many different employment opportunities in the defense industry that require varying degrees of education, background, skills, abilities, knowledge, and experience. Many seeking employment in the defense industry are often under the misconception that you must have a college degree, military or government experience, or special skills and experience to be considered for employment. The reality is that there are a number of opportunities available in this industry that are general in nature and require varying levels of education and experience. Opportunities are available for those with high school diploma and GED level educations to those with associates, bachelors, masters, and doctorate degrees. Employment opportunities scan the spectrum from clerical and custodial to management, manufacturing, legal, sales, construction, healthcare, engineering, security, technology, marketing,

1

training, human resources, operations, logistics, general labor, administrative, and scientific to name just a few. Full time, part time, contract, and telecommute (home office) opportunities are available. We have made every attempt to list companies that advertise multiple employment opportunities on a continuous basis. Many of the companies listed post new jobs daily so be sure to check often.

THE LIST

★

1, 2, 3 ...

★

1. **3M DEFENSE**
   www.3m.com

2. **21ct**
   www.21ct.com

4

★
A
★

3. ## AAI CORPORATION
www.aaicorp.com

4. ## AAR CORPORATION
www.aarcorp.com

5. ## ABM INDUSTRIES
www.abm.com

6. ## ACADEMI
www.academi.com

7. ## ACCENTURE
www.accenture.com

8. ## ACCUVANT
www.accuvant.com

9. ## ACS
www.acs-inc.com

10. ## ACTI
http://act-i.com

11. **ADS**
www.adsinc.com

12. **ADVANCIA**
www.advancia.com

13. **AECOM**
www.aecom.com

14. **AEROINDUSTRY JOBS**
www.aeroindustryjobs.com

15. **AEROJET**
www.aerojet.com

16. **AEROTEK**
www.aerotek.com

17. **AEROVIRONMENT**
www.aerovironment.com

18. **AFSC**
www.afsc-usa.com

19. **AGGREKO**
www.aggreko.com

20. **AGILITY DEFENSE & GOVERNMENT SERVICES**
www.agilitylogistics.com

21. **ARINC**
www.arinc.com

22. **AKIMA**
www.akima.com

23. **ALCOA DEFENSE**
www.alcoa.com/defense/en/home.asp

24. **ALION SCIENCE AND TECHNOLOGY**
www.alionscience.com/careers

25. **ALLIED BARTON**
www.alliedbarton.com

26. **ALLISON TRANSMISSION**
www.allisontransmission.com

27. **ALUTIIQ**
www.alutiiq.com

28. **AMELEX**
www.amelexinc.com

29. **AMERICAN SYSTEMS CORPORATION**
www.americansystems.com

30. **AMETEK AEROSPACE AND DEFENSE**
www.ametekaerodefense.com/careers

31. **ANAREN**
www.anaren.com

32. **ANSER**
www.anser.org

33. **APPLIED INDUSTRIAL TECHNOLOGIES**
www.applied.com

34. **ARMA**
www.arma-global.com

★

B

★

43. **BAE SYSTEMS**
www.baesystems.com

44. **BALL AEROSPACE & TECHNOLOGIES**
www.ballaerospace.com

45. **BARNES**
www.barnesacrospace.com

46. **BATTELLE**
http://battelle.org

47. **BECHTEL**
www.bechtel.com

48. **BEAVER AEROSPACE AND DEFENSE**
www.beaver-online.com

49. **BIZZELL CORPORATION**
www.bizzellcorp.com

50. **BOEING**
www.boeing.com

51. **BOOZ ALLEN HAMILTON**
www.boozallen.com

52. **BOSH GLOBAL SERVICES**
www.boshgs.com

53. **BOWHEAD SUPPORT SERVICE**
www.bowheadsupport.com

54. **BRTRC**
www.brtrc.com

★

C

★

55. **C2 ESSENTIALS**
www.c2essentials.com

56. **CACI**
www.caci.com

57. **CAE USA**
www.cae.com

58. **CAMBER CORPORATION**
www.camber.com

59. **CAMBRIDGE INTERNATIONAL SYSTEMS**
www.cbridge.org

60. **CAPE FOX CORPORATION**
www.capefoxcorp.com

61. **CAPSTONE CORPORATION**
www.capstonecorp.com

62. **CATERPILLAR**
www.cat.com

63. **CB&I**
www.cbi.com

64. **CDI CORPORATION**
www.cdicorp.com

65. **CELESTAR CORPORATION**
www.celestarcorp.com

66. **CGI FEDERAL**
www.cgi.com/en/careers

67. **CH2M HILL**
www.ch2m.com

68. **CHENEGA CORPORATION**
www.chenega.com

69. **CIRCOR**
www.circor.com

70. **COBHAM**
www.cobham.com

71. **COLSA**
www.colsa.com

72. **CONCURRENT TECHNOLOGIES CORPORATION**
www.ctc.com

73. **CRANE**
www.craneco.com

74. **CSC**
www.csc.com

75.   **CTS INTERNATIONAL**
      www.ctsinternational.com

76.   **CUBIC**
      www.cubic.com

77.   **CURTISS
      WRIGHT CONTROLS**
      www.cwcontrols.com

★

D

★

78. **D3 AIR AND SPACE OPERATIONS**
www.d3aso.com

79. **DAIMLER TRUCKS NORTH AMERICA**
www.daimler-trucksnorthamerica.com

80. **DANA HOLDING CORPORATION**
www.dana.com

81. **DAY AND ZIMMERMANN**
www.dayzim.com

82. **DCS CORPORATION**
www.dcscorp.com

83. **DEFENSE TALENT NETWORK**
www.defensetalent.com

84. **DELEX SYSTEMS**
www.delex.com

85. **DRC**
www.drc.com

86. **DRG**
www.drgok.com

87. **DRS TECHNOLOGIES**
www.drs.com

88. **DS2**
www.ds2.com

89. **DSCI**
www.dsci.com

90. **DUPONT COMPANY**
www.dupont.com

91. **DYNCORP INTERNATIONAL**
www.dyn-intl.com

92. **DYNETICS**
www.dynetics.com

★

E

★

93. ## E3 FEDERAL SOLUTIONS
www.e3federal.com

94. ## EATON CORPORATION
www.eaton.com

95. ## EAGLE SYSTEMS AND SERVICES
www.esascorp.com

96. ## ECS FEDERAL
www.ecsfederal.com

97. ## ELBIT SYSTEMS OF AMERICA
www.elbitsystems-us.com

98. ## EMCOR GROUP
www.emcorgroup.com

99. ## ENGILITY
www.engilitycorp.com

100. ## ENERSYS
www.enersys.com

101. EOIR TECHNOLOGIES
www.eoir.com

102. ESTERLINE DEFENSE TECHNOLOGIES
www.esterline.com

103. EVERGREEN AVIATION
www.evergreenaviation.com

★

F

★

104. **FCI FEDERAL**
http://fcifederal.com

105. **FEDSYS SECURE**
www.fedsys.com

106. **FEDERAL STAFFING RESOURCES**
www.fsrpeople.com

107. **FINMECCANICA**
www.finmeccanicausa.com

108. **FLIGHT SAFETY INTERNATIONAL**
www.flightsafety.com

109. **FLIR SYSTEMS**
www.flir.com

110. **FLUOR CORPORATION**
www.fluor.com

111. **FORCE 3**
www.force3.com

★

G

★

112. **G4S SECURITY**
http://www.g4s.us/en-US

113. **GE AVIATION**
www.geaviation.com

114. **GENERAL ATOMICS**
www.ga.com

115. **GENERAL DYNAMICS**
www.generaldynamics.com

116. **GOLDBELT INC.**
www.goldbelt.com

117. **GOODRICH CORPORATION**
www.goodrich.com

118. **GS5 LLC.**
www.gs5-llc.com

119. **GULFSTREAM**
www.gulfstream.com

★

H

★

120. **HALLIBURTON**
www.halliburton.com

121. **HARRIS CORPORATION**
www.harris.com

122. **HDT GLOBAL**
www.hdtglobal.com

123. **HENRY M. JACKSON FOUNDATION**
www.hjf.org

124. **HONEYWELL**
www.honeywell.com

125. **HUNTINGTON INGALLS INDUSTRIES**
www.huntingtoningalls.com

★

I

★

126. **i3**
www.i3-corps.com

127. **IAP WORLDWIDE SERVICES**
www.iapws.com

128. **IBIS TEK LLC**
www.ibistek.com

129. **IBM CORPORATION**
www.ibm.com/federal

130. **ICF INTERNATIONAL**
www.icfi.com

131. **IDEAL INNOVATIONS INC**
www.idealinnovations.com

132. **IDS INTERNATIONAL**
www.idsinternational.net

133. **IEM**
www.iem.com

134. **INCADENCE STARTEGIC SOLUTIONS**
www.incadencecorp.com

135. **INFINITY TECHNOLOGY**
www.itllc.com

136. **INSIGNA TECHNOLOGY SERVICES**
www.insigniatechnology.com

137. **INTERTEK**
www.intertek.com

138. **INTELLIGENT DECISIONS**
www.intelligent.net

139. **ITA INTERNATIONAL**
www.ita-intl.com

140. **ITT EXELIS**
www.exelisinc.com

141. **ITAC SOLUTIONS**
www.itacsolutions.com

★

J

★

142. **JACOBS TECHNOLOGY**
www.jacobstechnology.com

143. **JAMISON PROFESSIONAL SERVICES**
www.jps-online.net

144. **JMA SOLUTIONS**
www.jma-solutions.com

145. **J.M. WALLER ASSOCIATES**
www.jmwaller.com

146. **JOHNSON CONTROLS**
www.johnsoncontrols.com

147. **JORGE SCIENTIFIC**
www.jorge.com

148. **JS FIRM**
www.jsfirm.com

★

K

★

149. **KAEGAN CORPORATION**
www.kaegan.com

150. **KAMAN AEROSPACE**
www.kaman.com

151. **KBR**
www.kbr.com

152. **KEARFOTT CORPORATION**
www.kearfott.com

153. **KEARNEY AND COMPANY**
www.kearneyco.com

154. **KEYPOINT GOVERNMENT SOLUTIONS**
www.keypoint.us.com

155. **KEY LOGIC SYSTEMS**
www.keylogic.com

156. **KGS**
www.kforcegov.com

157. **KINGFISHER SYSTEMS**
www.kingfishersys.com

158. **KRATOS DEFENSE**
www.kratosdefense.com

★

L

★

159. **L-3 COMMUNICATIONS**
www.l-3com.com

160. **LANDMARK EARTH SOLUTIONS**
www.erosion-management.com

161. **LEIDOS**
www.leidos.com

162. **LEONIE GROUP**
www.leoniegroup.com

163. **LEUPOLD & STEVENS**
www.leupold.com

164. **LINCOLN MILITARY HOUSING**
www.lincolnmilitary.com

165. **LINXX GLOBAL SOLUTIONS**
www.linxxglobal.com

166. **LMI**
www.lmi.org

167. **LOCKHEED MARTIN CORPORATION**
www.lockheedmartin.com

168. **LORD CORPORATION**
www.lord.com

169. **LSI**
www.lsijax.com

★

M

★

170. **M2 SERVICES CORPORATION**
www.m2-services.com

171. **M.C. DEAN**
www.mcdean.com

172. **MACB**
www.macb.com

173. **MANAGEMENT CONCEPTS**
www.managementconcepts.com

174. **MAIN NERVE**
www.mainnerve.com

175. **MANCON**
www.manconinc.com

176. **MANTECH CORPORATION**
www.mantech.com

177. **MARKLOGIC CORPORATION**
www.marklogic.com

178. **MARVIN LAND SYSTEMS**
www.marvingroup.com

179. **MCKEAN DEFENSE GROUP**
www.mckean-defense.com

180. **MCR**
www.mcri.com

181. **MEGGITT**
www.meggitt.com

182. **MHN GOVERNMENT SERVICES**
www.mhngs.com

183. **MISSION ESSENTIAL PERSONNEL**
www.missionessential.com

184. **MISSION 1ST**
www.mission1st.com

185. **MOOG**
www.moog.com

186. **MORPHOTRUST USA**
www.morphotrust.com

187. **MTS**
www.mts-usa.com

188. **MTS TECHNOLOGIES**
www.mtstech.com

★

N

★

189. **NANA DEVELOPMENT CORPORATION**
www.nana.com

190. **NATIONAL GOVERNMENT SERVICES**
www.ngsservices.com

191. **NCI**
www.nciinc.com

192. **NETCENTRICS**
www.netcentrics.com

193. **NOBLE**
www.noblegov.com

194. **NORTHROP GRUMMAN**
www.northropgrumman.com

★

O

★

195. **OAKLEY**
www.oakley.com

196. **OASIS SYSTEMS**
www.oasissystems.com

197. **OCEANEERING INTERNATIONAL**
www.oceaneering.com

198. **OLGOONIK**
www.olgoonik.com

199. **OMNIPLEX**
www.omniplex.com

200. **OPTIMOS**
www.optimos.com

201. **OSHKOSH DEFENSE**
www.oshkoshdefense.com

202. **OSI SYSTEMS**
www.osi-systems.com

★

P

★

203. **PACIFIC SCIENTIFIC ENERGETIC MATERIALS**
www.psemc.com

204. **PAE**
www.pae.com

205. **PANASONIC SOLUTIONS**
www.panasonic.com/business-solutions

206. **PARSONS CORPORATION**
www.parsons.com

207. **PARKER HANNIFIN**
www.parker.com

208. **PATRICO ENTERPRISES**
www.patricioenterprises.com

209. **PELICAN PRODUCTS**
www.pelican.com

210. **PEOPLE TEC**
www.people-tec.com

211. **PHACIL**
www.phacil.com

212. **PHILLIPS SERVICE INDUSTRIES**
www.psi-online.com

213. **PICERNE MILITARY HOUSING**
www.corviasmilitaryliving.com

214. **PINNACLE MILITARY HOUSING**
www.pinnacleams.com

215. **PIONEER TECHNOLOGIES**
www.ptc-us.com

216. **PITON SCIENCE AND TECHNOLOGY**
www.pitonscience.com

217. **POLARIS INDUSTRIES**
www.polaris.com

218. **PLANATE MANAGEMENT GROUP**
www.planate.net

219. **PLANETECHS**
www.planetechs.com

220. **PLANNED SYSTEMS INTERNATIONAL**
www.plan-sys.com

221. **PPG INDUSTRIES**
www.ppg.com

222. **PPDG**
www.ppdg.com

223. **PROSOL**
www.prosol1.com

224. **PRIDE INDUSTRIES**
www.prideindustries.com

★

Q

★

225. **QUANTECH SERVICES**
www.quantechserv.com

226. **QUANTUM RESEARCH**
www.quantum-intl.com

227. **QTC MANAGEMENT**
www.qtcm.com

★

R

★

228. **RADIANCE TECHNOLOGIES**
www.radiancetech.com

229. **RAYTHEON**
www.raytheon.com

230. **RECRUIT VETERANS**
www.recruitveterans.com

231. **RED GATE GROUP**
www.redgategrp.com

232. **RIVERSIDE RESEARCH**
www.riversideresearch.org

233. **ROCKWELL COLLINS**
www.rockwellcollins.com

234. **RGS**
www.rgsinc.com

★
S
★

235. **S3 INC**
www.s3inc.com

236. **S4 INC**
www.s4inc.com

237. **SABRE SYSTEMS**
www.sabresystems.com

238. **SAIC**
www.saic.com

239. **SALIENT FEDERAL SOLUTIONS**
www.salientfed.com

240. **SANMINA SCI**
www.sanmina-sci.com

241. **SARGENT AEROSPACE AND DEFENSE**
www.sargentaerospace.com

242. **SAWDEY SOLUTION SERVICES**
www.sawdeysolutionservices.com

243. SCHAFER CORPORATION
www.schafercorp.com

244. SCIENTIFIC RESEARCH
CORPORATION
www.scires.com

245. SECURE MISSION SOLUTIONS
www.securemissionsolutions.com

246. SERCO
www.serco-na.com

247. SENTEL CORPORATION
www.sentel.com

248. SNC
www.sncorp.com

249. SIG SAUER
www.sigsauer.com

250. SIGMATEC
www.sigmatech.com

251. SIKORSKY
www.sikorsky.com

252. SILVERBACK 7
www.silverback7.com

253. SOS INTERNATIONAL
www.sosiltd.com

254. SOTERA DEFENSE
www.soteradefense.com

255. **SOUTHWEST RESEARCH INSTITUTE**
www.swri.org

256. **SRA INTERNATIONAL**
www.sra.com

257. **SRC INC**
www.srcinc.com

258. **SRI INTERNATIONAL**
www.sri.com

259. **STEWART AND STEVENSON**
www.stewartandstevenson.com

260. **STRATEGIC RESOURCES INC**
www.sri-hq.com

261. **STS INTERNATIONAL**
www.stsint.com

262. **STS SYSTEMS INTEGRATION**
www.ssi-anc.com

263. **SURVICE ENGINEERING**
www.survice.com

★
T
★

264. **TAD PGS**
www.tadpgs.com

265. **TAPESTRY SOLUTIONS**
www.tapestrysolutions.com

266. **TASC**
www.tasc.com

267. **TATITLEK CORPORATION**
www.tatitlek.com

268. **TE CONNECTIVITY**
www.te.com

269. **TECHWISE**
www.techwise.com

270. **TECH USA**
www.techusa.net

271. **TECHNICAL INNOVATION**
www.technical-innovation.com

272. **TELECOMMUNICATION SYSTEMS**
www.telecomsys.com

273. **TELEDYNE**
www.teledyne.com

274. **TELEPHONICS CORPORATION**
www.telephonics.com

275. **TELUM PROTECTION CORPORATION**
www.telumcorp.com

276. **TETRA TECH**
www.tetratech.com

277. **TEXTRON SYSTEMS**
www.textronsystems.com

278. **THE CENTECH GROUP**
www.centechgroup.com

279. **THE GENEVA FOUNDATION**
www.genevausa.org

280. **THE HINKLE GROUP**
www.hinklegroup.net

281. **THE MACALAN GROUP**
www.themacalangroup.com

282. **THREAT SQUAD**
www.threatsquad.com

283. **TREMCO INC**
www.tremcoroofing.com

284. **TRI-COR INDUSTRIES**
www.tricorind.com

285. **TRIPLE CANOPY**
www.triplecanopy.com

286. **TROFHOLZ TECHNOLOGIES**
www.tti-tech.com

287. **TYBRIN**
www.tybrin.com

288. **TYCO**
www.tyco.com

★

U

★

289. **UNITED HEALTH GROUP**
www.unitedhealthgroup.com

290. **UNITED TECHNOLOGIES**
www.utc.com

291. **UNIVERSAL SERVICES OF AMERICA**
www.universalpro.com

292. **URS**
www.urs.com

293. **USFALCON**
www.usfalcon.com

V

294. **VALBIN CORPORATION**
www.valbin.org

295. **VIASAT**
www.viasat.com

296. **VSE CORPORATION**
www.vsecorp.com

297. **VT GROUP**
www.vt-group.com

298. **VYKIN CORPORATION**
www.vykincorp.com

W

299. **W.L. GORE AND ASSOCIATES**
www.gore.com

300. **W.W. WILLIAMS LOGISTICS**
www.wwwilliams.com

301. **WALDEN SECURITY**
www.waldensecurity.com

302. **WHITNEY BRADLEY & BROWN**
www.wbbinc.com

303. **WINN COMPANIES**
www.winncompanies.com

304. **WYLE AEROSPACE**
www.wyle.com

X Y Z

305. **XLA**
www.xla.com

www.ingramcontent.com/pod-product-compliance
Lightning Source LLC
Chambersburg PA
CBHW071810170526
45167CB00003B/1250